independent cymbal rhythms

by
bobby williams

Edited by Rick Mattingly

ISBN 978-1-4803-6457-8

HAL•LEONARD®
CORPORATION
7777 W. BLUEMOUND RD. P.O. BOX 13819 MILWAUKEE, WI 53213

In Australia Contact:
Hal Leonard Australia Pty. Ltd.
4 Lentara Court
Cheltenham, Victoria, 3192 Australia
Email: ausadmin@halleonard.com.au

Visit Hal Leonard Online at
www.halleonard.com

contents

Preface 4

Introduction 4

Practice Tips 5

Chapter 1A: Driving quarter notes 6

Chapter 1B: Quarter-note and eighth-note cymbal rhythms 8

Chapter 2: Sixteenth notes on cymbal 12

Chapter 3: Syncopated cymbal rhythms 16

Chapter 4: Triplets 20

Chapter 5: 12/8 feel 26

Chapter 6: Thirty-second note grooves 32

Chapter 7: Triplets and thirty-seconds 34

Chapter 8: Grace notes 36

Chapter 9: Alternating hi-hat 38

Chapter 10: Rock and smooth jazz grooves 40

preface

This book is designed to give drummers the ability to develop their right or left hand, whichever they use for cymbal or hi-hat, combined with different snare and bass drum rhythms.

The various cymbal rhythms will help develop your cymbal hand to play almost any rhythm, or changes in cymbal rhythms, that you may encounter. Coordinating different cymbal rhythms with different bass and snare drum rhythms can prove challenging! My hope is this book will exercise your coordination and stimulate your mind while developing the cymbal hand.

Please experiment with combining the exercises for even more possibilities. Playing eighth notes all the time can soon become boring to you and your audience. Expand your abilities and open new horizons for yourself. Remember, playing drums is not just physical, but also a good workout for your mind!

Special thanks to fellow teacher John Walker for helping me reach my dreams.

introduction

Welcome to *Independent Cymbal Rhythms*! This book is designed for the advancing and advanced drummer, written to challenge you both physically and mentally.

I have spent almost my entire life as a professional drummer and teacher and have been privileged to study with some of the country's best drummers, either in person or through their publications. As good as they were, I felt some things could be improved upon or were not addressed at all. With this in mind, I've written this book.

Whereas many drummers can play sophisticated bass drum/snare drum grooves, they often maintain steady quarter notes, eighth notes, or sixteenth notes on the ride cymbal or hi-hat throughout a song. The exercises in this book are designed to free up your ride playing so you can achieve greater rhythmic variety in your grooves.

The exercises in this book are also designed to develop endurance, coordination, flexibility, and finesse of movement—all qualities of a good drummer! Practicing my exercises thoroughly will help you achieve your full potential as a drummer and hopefully get you thinking of other rhythmic possibilities!

—Bobby

practice tips

The exercises in this book are notated for ride cymbal, snare drum, and bass drum. You can substitute the cymbal cup or hi-hat for the ride cymbal to produce interesting variations.

When you encounter a particularly challenging exercise, practice it part by part, starting with the cymbal (see example 1A below). Then add straight quarter notes on the bass drum (example 1B). When you are comfortable with that, revert to the original bass rhythm (example 1C). Finallly, add the snare drum (example 1D).

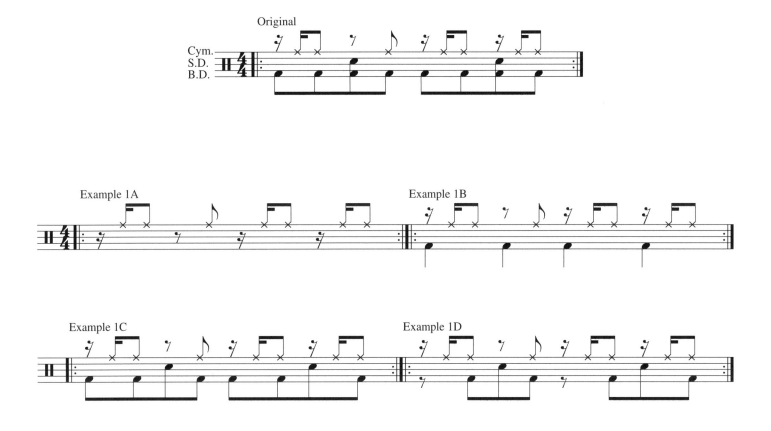

Chapter 1A
Driving quarter notes

Suggested application: medium to heavy rock and Latin grooves

This section is based on driving quarter notes on the cup of the ride cymbal. Emphasis is on a good, solid rock drive. Go slowly with these beats at first and get a feel for them. Play these beats along with music, if possible.

In exercises 21–24, start by playing the cymbal variations with quarter notes on the bass drum, until the cymbal rhythms become easy to play. Then play the patterns as written.

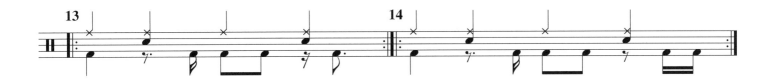

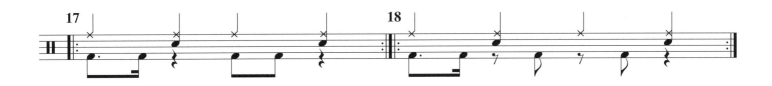

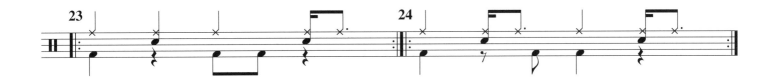

Chapter 1B
Quarter-note and eighth-note cymbal rhythms

Suggested application: medium to heavy rock and Latin grooves

Finger and wrist action is very important when you play these rhythms on hi-hat or ride. Practice slowly at first. Play bass notes as cleanly as possible when they are grouped in threes or fours. You may need to adjust your foot on the bass pedal to sustain an even flow with the sixteenth notes.

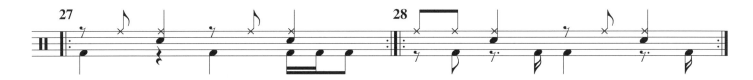

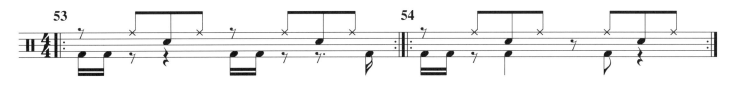

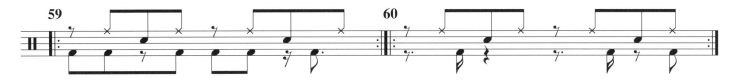

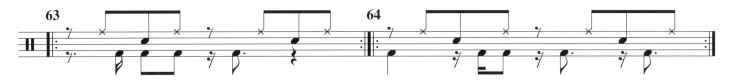

Chapter 2
Sixteenth notes on cymbal

Suggested application: light to medium rock, smooth jazz, salsa, and Jamaican

Use the tip of the sticks on the hi-hat or ride cymbal to get a better bounce for the sixteenth notes.

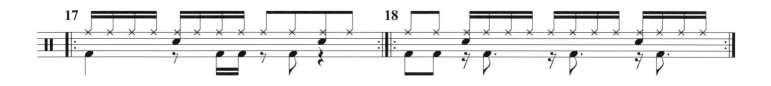

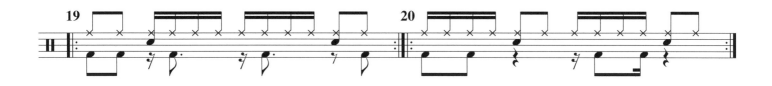

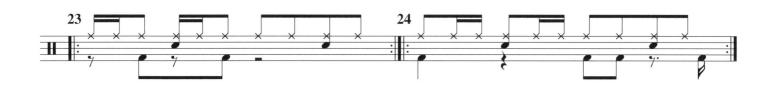

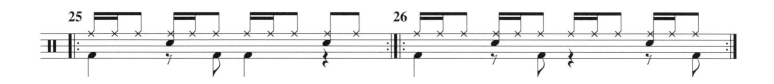

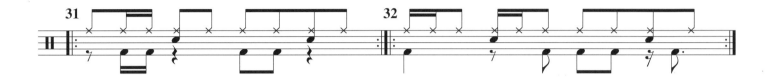

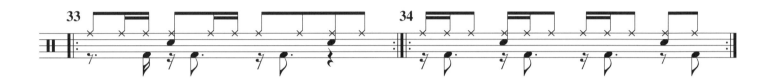

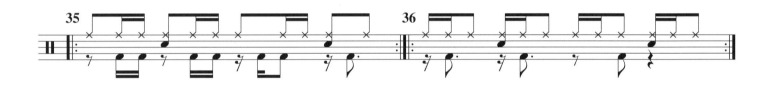

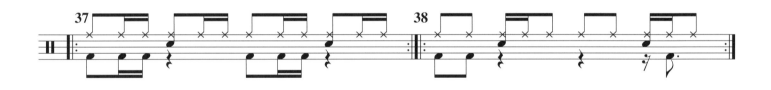

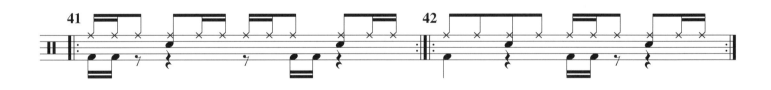

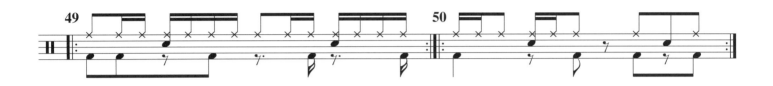

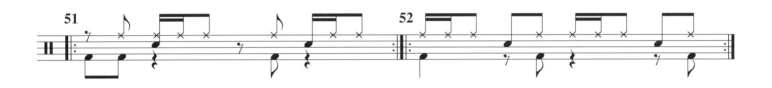

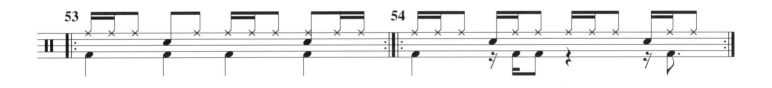

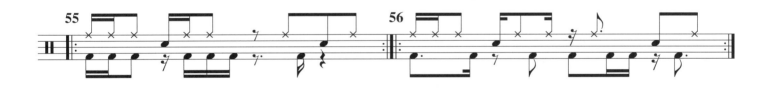

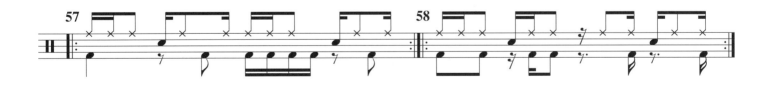

Chapter 3
Syncopated cymbal rhythms
Suggested application: rock, Latin, and smooth jazz

Coordination development is the key here. Tight wrist and finger control and clarity are a must.

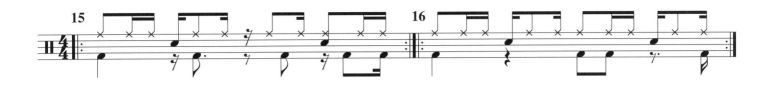

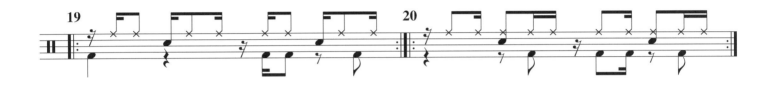

Optional: omit bass drum on beat 4.

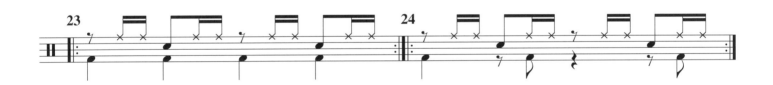

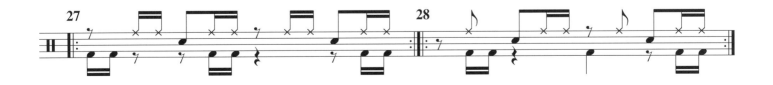

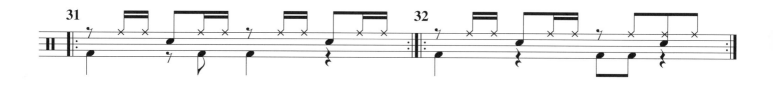

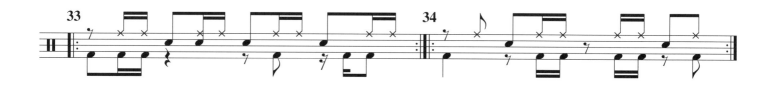

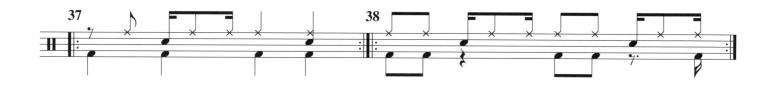

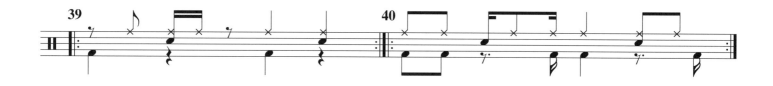

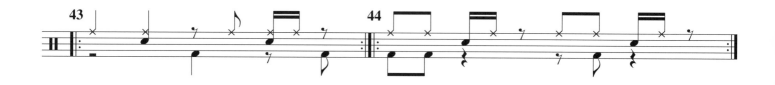

Optional: add a cymbal note to the "and" of beat 4.

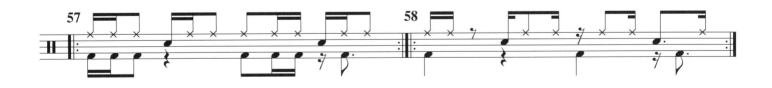

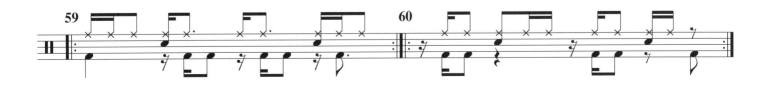

Chapter 4
Triplets

Suggested application: light rock, funk, and smooth jazz

Wrist action is very important here. You want to produce a sound with your drumstick that is bright and quick. Play the hi-hat/ride cymbal rhythms with just the snare before adding the bass. To create different beats, add bass drum notes where rests are notated.

Play bass notes as cleanly as possible when they are grouped in threes or fours. You may need to adjust your foot on the bass pedal to sustain an even flow with the sixteenth notes.

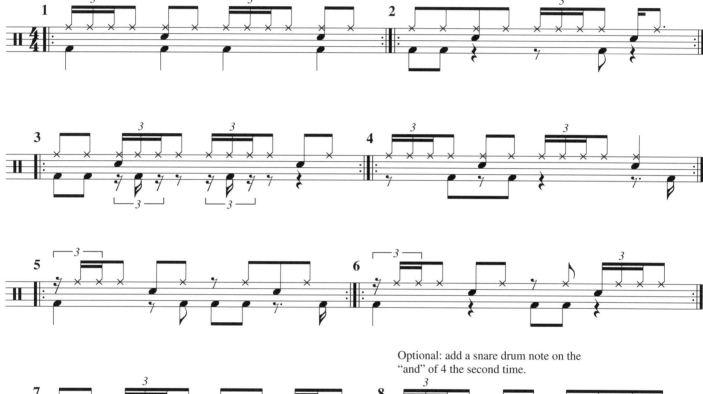

Optional: add a snare drum note on the "and" of 4 the second time.

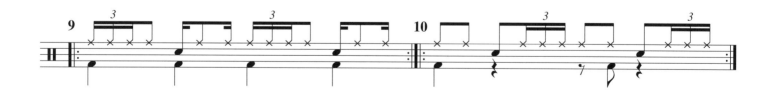

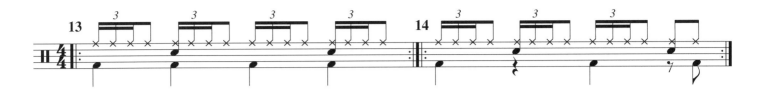

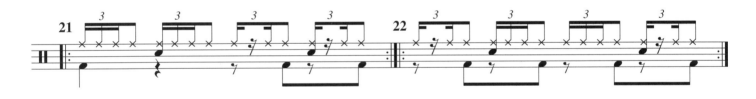

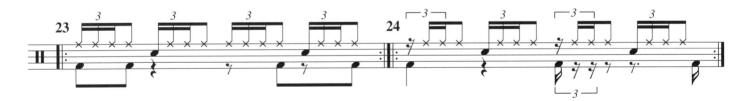

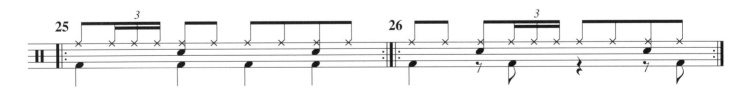

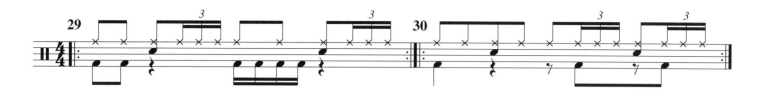

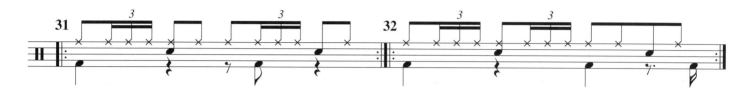

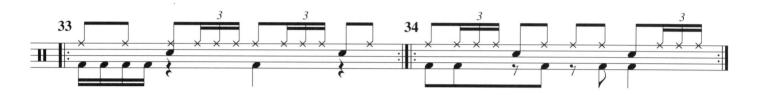

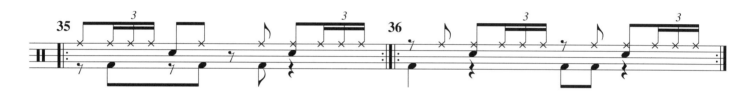

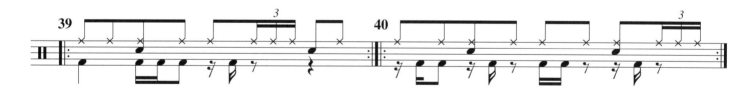

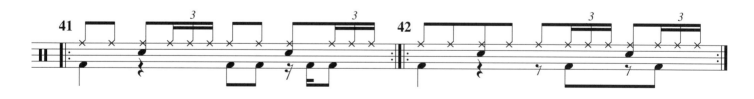

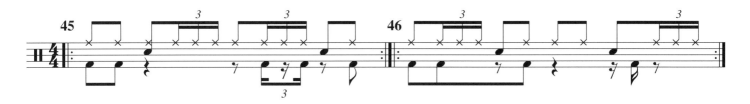

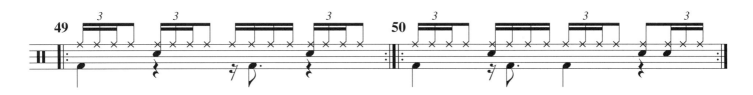

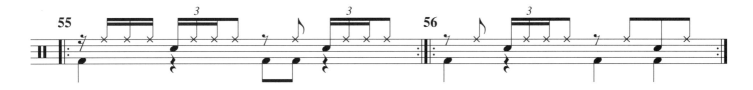

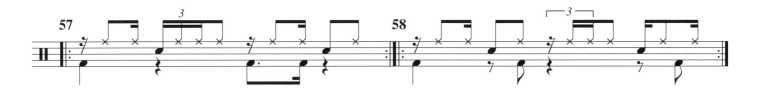

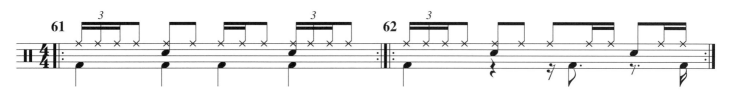

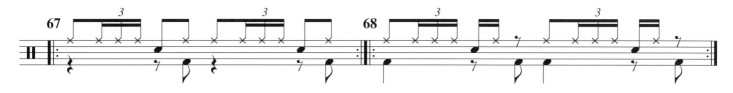

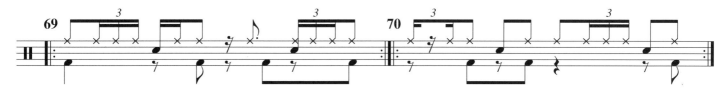

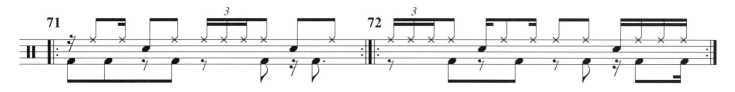

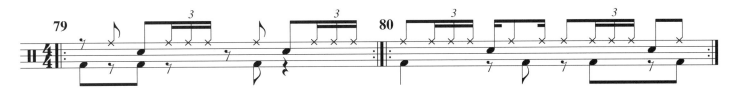

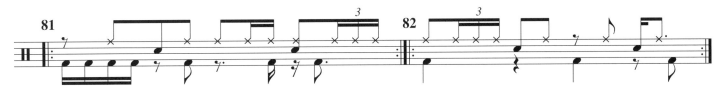

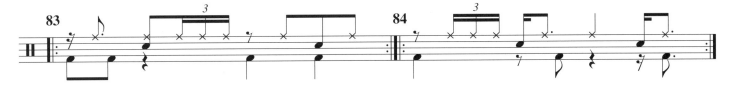

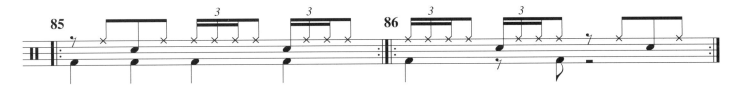

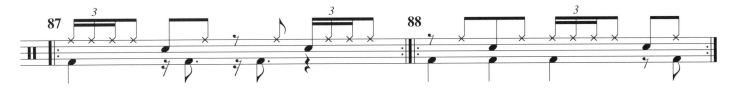

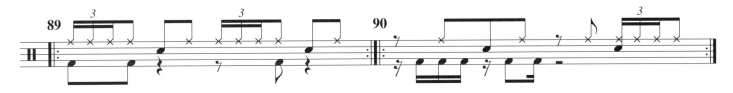

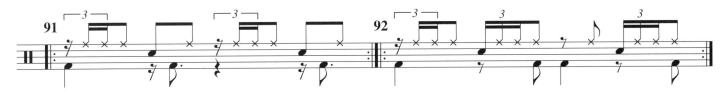

Chapter 5
12/8 feel

Suggested application: blues and jazz grooves

Most of the exercises in this chapter are written in 12/8 time, which is essentially the same as a triplet feel
in 4/4. These beats can be used for one measure of a song or for multiple measures throughout the song.
Practice these exercises in slow to medium tempos, and practice with music if possible.

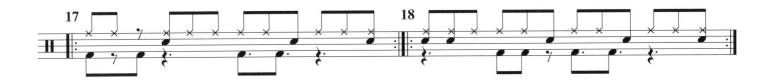

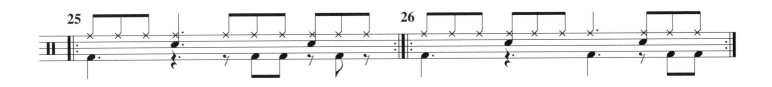

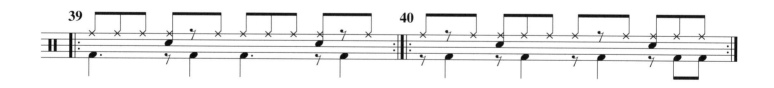

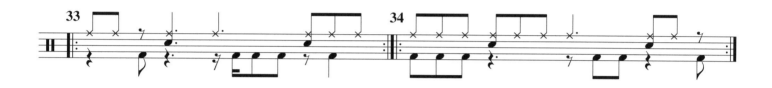

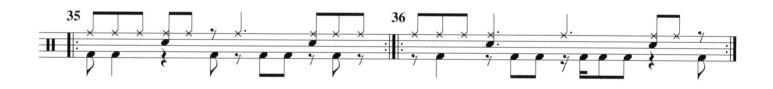

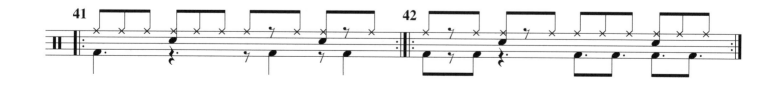

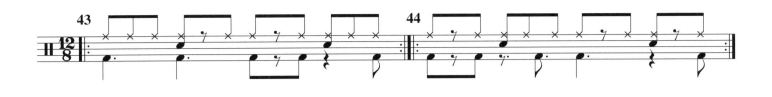

Optional: omit the last cymbal note.

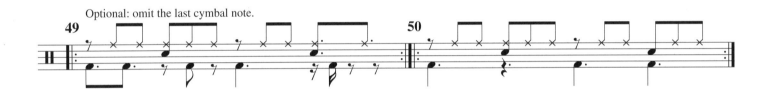

Optional: add a snare drum on beat 3.

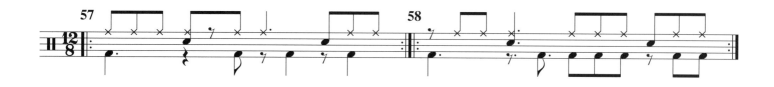

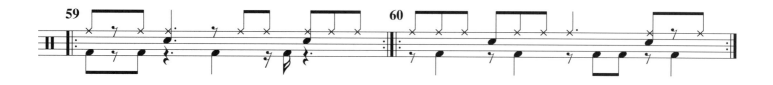

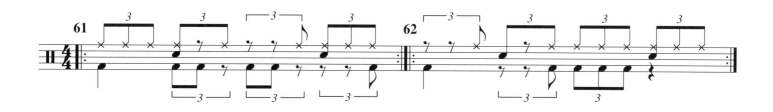

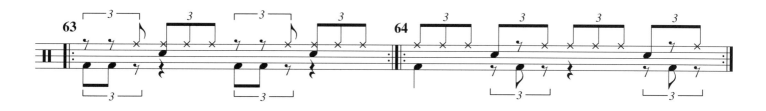

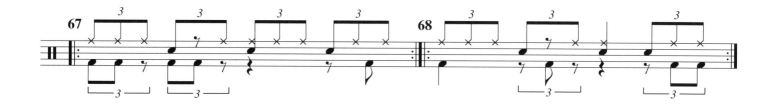

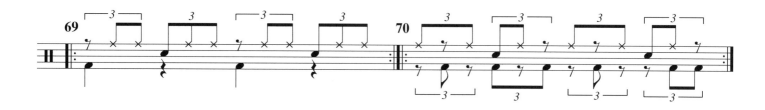

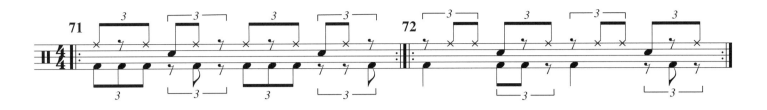

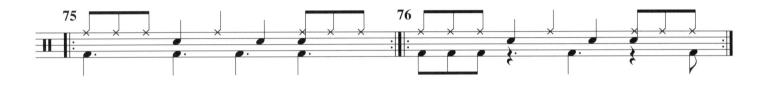

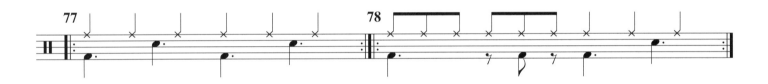

Chapter 6
Thirty-second note grooves

Suggested application: techno/disco grooves

Watch the tempo; not too fast. Play very lightly with both sticks alternating on the hi-hat. Play all notes very cleanly. Play with the tip or shoulder of the stick to get the sound you want. Work on the hi-hat or small ride cymbal close to snare first.

Optional: the second time through,
play bass drum on 1 or 1 "and."

In the following exercises, you can play bass drum where rests are notated to create additional patterns.

Chapter 7
Triplets and thirty-seconds

*Suggested application: slower tempo jazz-rock and
smooth jazz with a touch of techno*

Alternate both sticks on the hi-hat. Finger control is essential. Play smoothly, cleanly and be exact. Play
quarter notes on the bass drum first, then add the different bass note combinations.

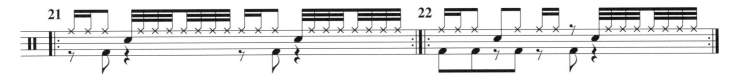

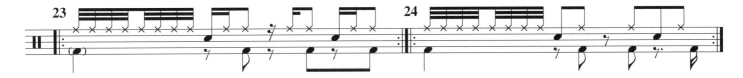

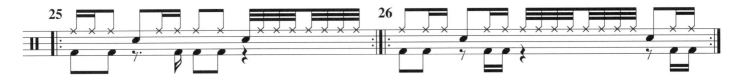

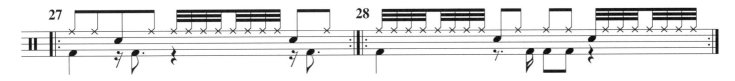

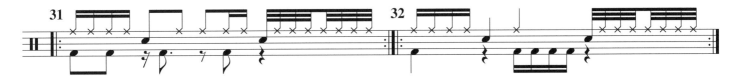

Chapter 8
Grace notes

Suggested application: light rock or jazz-rock, smooth jazz, or techno or disco

Grace notes add color and uniqueness; pay special attention to the clarity of notes. Alternate both sticks on the hi-hat.

Chapter 9
Alternating hi-hat

Suggested application: Caribbean or salsa grooves

Alternate both hands on hi-hat for delicate sounds in rock, smooth jazz, etc. Some grooves can be played with one hand on the hi-hat. Practice cymbal and snare first, or practice the first two counts, then the last two counts.

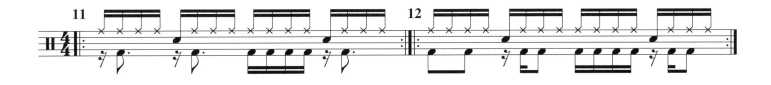

Chapter 10
Rock and smooth jazz grooves

Suggested application: rock or smooth jazz grooves

Here are six rock/smooth jazz grooves with unique cymbal and bass rhythms.